the shape of my will

by Graham Cwinn

*"I only believe in
one thing
that my profound power will not restore me
but will establish me
myself
Antonin Artaud
so as to know myself, feel myself, desire myself."*
— Antonin Artaud

"And these death sensations laid out end to end, this suffocation, this despair, these spells of drowsiness, this desolation, this silence — don't we see them in the enlarged suspension of a dream, with the feeling that one of the faces of a new reality is perpetually looking over our shoulder?"
—Antonin Artaud

"This is your life, and it's ending one minute at a time. Once we have realized this, our personal heaven is at our fingertips. The mist of boredom will clear away if we only dare to scare away the grotesque ghost of a life laid out in front of us..."
— The Ocean Collective

"It is not necessary that you leave the house. Remain at your table and listen. Do not even listen, only wait. Do not even wait, be wholly still and alone. The world will present itself to you for its unmasking, it can do no other, in ecstasy it will writhe at your feet."
— Franz Kafka

for those who ache.

Crawl Inside
(2020)

"one day all this will end."
(2021)

IN SICKNESS AND IN DEATH
(2021)

the need to construct a new reality
(2022)

the profound ecstasy of being
(2022)

Crawl Inside

I.

Hospital

my life is a hospital, stagnant and paranoid.
I can never seem to leave -- always returning
more fractured than before. a lifetime of
broken bones is nothing compared to being
stripped of my personality.

begging them not to take my clothes away.

"being outside for one hour at a time is a
privilege. being yourself is a privilege."

I etched a copper simulacrum
to convince them I am well enough
to go home

but I am not okay.

clutching suicidal thoughts and psychosis
like precious idols. gazing out the window
with revulsion, each face making my stomach
churn. soon I will be condemned to pace
that dismal hall again -- no different than
the ones in my mind.

season of drought

madness eats my skull.
misery and hunger
gnaw at my abdomen.
there will be no meals
today or tomorrow.
too embarrassed
to accept dinner invitations.
unable to provide for myself
or the ones I love.
a burden.
an affliction.

self-loathing feeds
this empty machine.

schizoaffective

i.

the last of my olanzapine
never balanced
clever phalanx of delusion
lays siege to neurons
voices scrape inside me

withdraw from the world
find a bridge to hang my noose
blood colder than Lake Ontario

Deluge

floating further away. there is just the sky and empty halls that you wander alone. this room is all you know, and your bed, and neither shed a single stroke of comfort anymore.

a deluge soaks into your brain.
instances fade like old polaroids.

it's rained in here for days and years. the sky turned grey and is falling to pieces. an ocean between us, now. on this island of scattered words I excavate the shore; gather sand from all our brightest days; send it to you in bottles that drift in the tide.

ich trage diese Krankheit bis ins Grab

mental illness is a dead body that I lug around with me. splayed on my floor, a bag over its head so I don't have to see that contorted face -- those glazed eyes. on the rare occasion that a friend comes over I stuff it into the closet. if I need to go out I wrap it in a spare rug and cellophane to pretend that I'm industrious and care about the interior design of my home. it looks absurd and it's hard to navigate through traffic but no one's noticed yet. I fear they might get a whiff of decaying tissue as I pass, or an icy hand will slump out, potentially tripping someone. I don't want anyone to get hurt. in my spare time I browse the internet for vacant graves or a corpse dumping site but I haven't had any luck.

trauma // night terrors

sinking down to suffer with the buried things. losing weight. losing sleep. drifting through endless weeks. cautious glances and whispers as I wait for the elevator.

"it's him -- he's the one that screams in the night."

broken wrist -- surgery, haikus, tedium

i.

torrential downpour
morphine daze obscures the time
lost in summer storms

atrophied muscles
tendons barely functional
stitches are itching

watch from darkened rooms
as birds hatch and flowers bloom
weary of this form

ii.

haikus are useless
attempts to appease the void
churning within me

anxious nights in bed
shaking off futility
it's a losing war.

there is a hole in
my chest - slowly eroding
- never shall I rest

iii.

please distract me from
boredom and my agony.
my bones are screaming.

no unified self
I can't function in this world
I just want to sleep

unable to draw
or paint or play piano
or clean the dishes

another grey day
contemplating suicide
will I have the strength?

"you make my chest implode."

blankets of ice
tuck me in with pneumonia

dreams. kissing
sand at the bottom of the river

as it holds my
breath in trembling hands.

cycles

i.

mania becomes unstoppable.
eating and sleeping are irrelevant.
swarming thoughts -- clarity
lost -- carried away to their hive.

blood rushes with euphoria.
anxiety twists into paranoia.

I can't control my anger.

watching myself burn
every bridge that I care about.

ii.

now I have turned to stone.
depression's rivers erode
my insides and spill into
every crevice. paralyzed
by despondency.
the belief that I am unworthy
of love. the certainty
that this will kill me.
a patient noose waits
under my bed -- biding
its time. it will be there
for me when I need
it most.

there is no relief. this will follow me
until the end. I will die from this.

I collapse and reform perpetually.

empty.

the sky is clear and blue.
sunshine and a gentle breeze.
people I will never understand.
I twist my mouth into a smile
and pretend to be one of them.

DIFFERENT ROADS TO THE SAME HELL

```
w                                       i
h                       b           e       n
e           f           l           r       s
n           o           a           u       i
                        c           t       d
y           s           k           n           e
o           l                       e
u           l           n           v       i
            e           e                   s
s       w               s           o
t                                   t       t
a           o           w                   o
r           t           h           t
e           n           e           a       m
    i                   r           h       e
                        e           t       e
                                            t
                    m           d
                    y           n       a           h
                                a       b           t
                e               t       s       a
            y                   s       u       e
            e                   r       r       d
        s                       e       d
                                d       i           n
        s                       n       t           i
        h                       u       y           a
        o                                           t
        u               ,               a           r
            l           e               n       e
            d           b               d       c
```

January

frost bites my spine as I try to shrug off 40 reasons
to give up on a cold, January night. they howl
in my ears and dull the sound of passing traffic;
hungrily sink into my raw, bruised forearm;
invade my body with a thousand piercing eyes.

learning to bear the thought of crowded
streets and eye contact with strangers.

clinging to warmth. the feeling is gone.
I did not expect to live this long.

this disorder

I'm fucking depressed and hallucinating.
I go for days without talking to a single person.

the maladaptive nature of this
disorder is profound. nothing
feels real. socially withdrawn
and unable to maintain contact.

the brink of homelessness. the gaze of suicide.
I refuse to succumb to another overdose -- I'd rather die
sober and insane. medications ineffective.
therapy provides little comfort.

I'm barely surviving.

psychosis

reaching into my pocket for a bit of change,
enough for that last meal. but all I pull out
are chameleons with twisted, cruel masks
that shift between ominous hues.
as I stumble down this corridor they stalk
me, camouflaged, jabbing me with their tongues
like sharp, tensile proboscides:
draining me of life,
my sanity.
the blood loss and weakening of mental
stamina have forced me to communicate
with beings from other dimensions, intimately
and intricately weaved into the threads of my mind.
another consciousness has invaded
my brain, slowly and meticulously
deconstructing me -- fragments
cast aside to sink into the bottomless
chasm.

I can see a world hidden behind ours,
carefully clothed and virgin to us.
to witness its naked essence is to instil
the punitive awe and terror
of the sublime.
tears are forming in reality's fabric:
chaos enters in the form of wolves
with octopi for tongues
and a semi-transmogrification of the self.
my head is a portable camping stove,
no eyes but the Flame to illuminate this strange place
from whence there is no return.

I spiral further into oblivion
-- never reaching the end.

wasting away // wasted days

restless teeth chew my lips.
insides on fire but the sweat
from my face turns to ice;
rips holes in my pathetic origami.

fumbling hands - torn paper - throw it away.

April [catatonia]

unrelenting torpor.
debilitating.
feverish haze swirls
behind vacant eyes.
a burning inside my head
(frayed wires; short circuits).
a dark detachment,
estranging me
from all that was once
familiar -- whether
the warmth of the sun
(smiling faces, tender
words) or this
all-consuming
anguish.

how to lose friends and alienate people.

haunted by illness. scarred from trauma.
anger seeps into everything. I carry the guilt
of bleeding on people who have never cut me.
I can only atone by altering my behaviour.

daily struggles
devoted to change.
reminding myself what it means
to be a decent fucking human being.

I take my medications every day.
I convince myself to eat. I walk outside
in the daylight. I'm honest in
psychotherapy.

I'm tired of this anger. I'm tired of bleeding
on people who have never cut me.

Shatter

I hope to see you Sunday (some day) .. acquiescent
to accumulated cracks - spreading like rivers,
or webs - we will crumble and smash
on rocks. liberated from
heavy bodies
made of
clay.

the crippling isolation

abandoned to the heat of summer. mental illness rules my home. writhing in sweat-soaked sheets. dreaming of rice fields and azure skies. perpetuating a cycle of self-injury. begrudging reliance on disability. a worried family that I haven't seen in months.

I will carry this disease to my grave.

schizoaffective

ii.

disruption of synaptic and syntactic frequencies
-- communication breaks down -- semantics
a distant dream.

degraded by this sickness
that is now more real than me.

a futile attempt to hang myself.
bruises on my neck for weeks.

the *Other* s   s
            m   e
               i   l

and cackles maniacally --
living within me -- finally free.

sun. ache. trudge.

I shrink from the sun for fear of it melting my
skin of wax
because I am a candle
and my flame has almost spent its course
pushing me out of myself until I am
no more
flesh drips with heat
grasping for even a single piece of myself
but I am w e a k
I shrink from the sun for fear of it melting my
skin of wax

dragging sedated feet towards
a vague notion of recovery.

It.

It shrieks from all sides. everything has become an enemy: the desk, the walls, even the sky. It is what makes getting up in the morning impossible. It is what makes eating breakfast impossible. It always watches from other people's eyes. It is what keeps you awake at night. It is what takes over your mind when gone unchecked. It is what makes you beg for the end. It is what takes away the strength to destroy yourself. It has crippled and enslaved you.

It is that paper face staring back from
cold glass. It is the fake skin hanging
from your bones. It has tunnelled
this yawning abyss that sits in your
chest. It is speaking to you from
within me, even now, moving my
hands away from yours. It is the
pill-coloured smiles pulling you through
each exhausting day. Its jittering jaws
devour your heart, rattle this cage of pale,
exposed ribs.

It gnashes Its teeth, gnawing your being. It has persisted for decades. It will continue to hollow you out. only a husk remains. shuffling aimlessly down hallways that are increasingly unfamiliar. a million ways to describe It. concede that It will forever be unnamed.

Lamotrigine

numb and detached after years of seeking shelter
from this storm. pleading for the strength to expire.
manic depression dismantles and abandons every
ambition. teeth rot in steady synchronicity.

I trudge into the strange darkness of tomorrow.
will the clouds part to illuminate a renewed purpose?
or instil me with quietude?

crawl inside

a rough feeling
as the rope snaps back

can't breathe

           can't see

thrashing and convulsing, hideous contortions

```
I never knew            mu
it                        ch.
would         so
      hurt
```

```
the b    an
    r    c
         h
```

cr / ac / ks

and

I crumple to grass and earth.
it didn't work. too hurt to try again.

retreat further into myself.
broken and ashamed.

schizoaffective

iii.

wandering empty streets.
afraid to return to my home.
tangled thoughts cast ripples in my perception.
each   dissociated   step takes me farther away from every-
thing. my cough echoes for fifteen minutes.

"I can't do this anymore."

I lay down in the ditch. curl up next to a pile
of old newspapers. sleep.

"all the oceans we contain, coming to light"

I dream of breezy vistas -- mazes of wind swept
corridors between brightly coloured buildings
by the sea.

salted air billows about and each
smiling face reminds me of you.

 the crashing of surf on rocks
fills my ears as I envision you here
in my arms, watching the sun sink
into the waves.

II.

The Stranger

there is someone in my home.

I sit in the living room listening
to the hush of their footsteps
as they haunt the hallway and
linger in the kitchen.

intermittently
they peek around the corner
and watch me -- silently
-- with twisted hands
and awful eyes.

on the third night they break
this terrible monotony and
step across the threshold.

I cower in the corner, frantically
waving my knife.

the only blood drawn is my own.

by morning they have vanished
-- another piece of me taken
in the night. I wait in bandaged
horror for their return.

there is someone in my home.
there is no one in my home.

avolition

I have lost the will to tend to these wounds.
the voices tell me it is all in vain. my mind
has shattered like glass on marble. schizoaffective
disorder has ruined me. I can't work, or pay my bills,
or prepare meals, or go outside.

I have failed as a person.

today I learned to fly

the urge to leave my body becomes reality. mesmerized, I watch myself break apart into a flock of starlings. swirling through the skies, I soar above houses and cars.

I settle in the cemetery; a few of me seek shade in the trees while the rest of me peck at the grass for insects and seeds.

I return with dismay to my human form and walk back to my apartment.

the bathroom mirror is in shards -- blood everywhere -- I look down and my arms are covered with gashes.

crisis

"are you at risk of harming yourself?"

"do you have an active plan?"

"how frequent are your hallucinations?"

"are you still hearing voices?"

"it will be several hours before
you can see the psychiatrist."

"I'm sorry but you will have to sit
in the waiting room."

"try to remain calm."

"the psychiatrist has decided that
he doesn't need to see you."

"we hope you get well soon."

windowpane

discomfort inhabits this room
as we stare out the window.

we stay silent. our eyes meet briefly before
the gaze di ss o l v e s

into embarrassed avoidance.

imagining a world of happiness; pretending there
isn't a void between us that can never be crossed.

diffident

falling

away

      from

         everyone

and

everything.

soon there will be

nothing left of me.

you keep pulling me through the days but I just want to stop and catch my breath and embrace the silence; I'm worn and drenched with these heavy rains of fatigue

"I'm okay."

"don't worry about me."

lies to help me scrape through the day. I question if I should talk about those horrible voices, or these constant suicidal thoughts. is it faux pas to begin a discourse on the phantoms that stalk every moment of my waking life?

"I'll be fine."

you see my still form and assume I have finally fallen asleep -- but my eyes are chiseled open, transfixed by the tumultuous dread that threatens to en gu lf and splinter me.

"I'm afraid of tomorrow."

"...our hands battered by the clutch of holding on."

you embrace the world with alacrity

despite the struggle in your weary

gaze. even the face of death

is weathered by your

passion.

the burden will become lighter.

trees and flowers will sprout

from your wounds.

descending into an illusion

reality twists and bends around me.
shifting patterns; vivid colours; sharing
thoughts with another mind.

I don't understand how people live.
just the idea of leaving my bed
induces panic attacks. lost in a schism
between my world and yours.

I can't be just this anymore.

eyes wide shut

it feels like yesterday:
that tight nervousness,
       sweating with anticipation,
waiting for a   push in the wrong
direction.

with desperate gulps I take in
all that harsh, liquid death.

drink.
drink.
drink.

I drown in perfect nothingness -- slipping
into nonbeing. but I am ripped from that
ocean of comfort and forced to once
again carry out this tiring, repetitive
routine you all worship as existence.

deep in my mind I'm still in that hospital bed
and you're sitting in the corner with a teary
face waiting to hear my voice just one last
time, and I'm doing everything I possibly
can to stop these eyes from opening again.

I admire your tenacity.
- for S.

you are discovering your
true being -- it shines brighter
than the sun. all shadows
will pale in your wake.

through the picture box and beyond

there is an endless canyon of static
between myself and the world.

bewildering visions are coming to life.

scarecrows step out of the television
and wait adamantly, eagerly, for me
to walk with them into

the 10th sub level of preposterousness.

hearing voices.

whispers fill my ears.

"you don't deserve to live."

the Other plants images
in my mind. telepathic
messages reverberate
in my skull.

"you belong to us."

I leave a letter for my loved ones.
this time I will not fail.

the voices create a passage and I follow them.

*become more than this
debilitating sickness --
learn to love yourself.*

"one day all this will end."

I.

Aripiprazole

these injections, in theory, should
alleviate my perpetual psychosis.

but

I've grown accustomed to the varying
brush strokes that make up the sky.
pastels and gouache today; will
it be watercolours tomorrow?
or acrylic?

will the world continue to be
a beautiful painting?

vibrancy

ecstasy
my blood surges
to the rhythm of your memory

breathless
staggering into the light
that radiates from you.

thus proclaimed the expanse known as Sky

the faint scratching of fabric against fabric.

hands feel every inch of my body.
I don't know whom they belong to.

what if they are disembodied?

I hear the clicking of eyelashes,
as if something (someone)
were able to see through this
darkness.

acrimonious doubts
cascade and splinter
on my back.

"what is the point of this?
why cling to life, only to
languish throughout
strained years?"

within myself I sense a flicker,
nearly imperceptible, enough
to keep these shadows at bay.

"I'll give myself three days to feel better."

hands grip the wheel. unable to stay between the li(n)es.
I contemplate driving off the overpass; sinking into the river.

needles(s)

I stopped injecting heroin -- it was exacerbating my hopelessness. mania. depression. psychosis. I drift between episodes. I try to take care of myself but I'm more alive in my dreams.

separation

vows of "I will always love you" and "I can't go on like this" stumble down the hall and out the door. resigned footsteps reverberate in the stairwell. your smiles elude me each morning; my hand searches the cold space where you laid next to me.

body dysmorphia

rolls of medication fat.
rotten teeth.

the smell of my sweaty
skin is nauseating.

I hide from the only
mirror in my house.

"he dreamt of Bones last night. I dreame of the Sunne."

beautiful creatures in remission,
striving to be absolved from this
misconception of our submission.

twitch and seethe beneath woven flesh.
your calcified prison shall schism like a cocoon.

shed these years of grief; raise your tired eyes
and see the sun as if for the first time.

enamel

grind the pills, grind the resin
from your spoon; grind your
teeth to stop your shaking
hands. don't
think about
your itchy
skin. don't
think about
the person
standing in
your hall.
don't think
about the
knife on
the table.
don't think
about visiting
the dentist.
don't think
about living
a
l
o
n
e
.

a little bitter

i.

I will never sleep in this psychiatric ward. patients are screaming.

in the morning I am served bowls of cereal and medication.

the walls are bending, the hallway floor is rippling; voices in my head

these thoughts aren't my own: they are placed there by someone who isn't real.

ii.

my bed is growling in threatening
yellow shades. it demands my flesh.

my green wrist band is how I get
outside. don't let them take it from me.

nothing to do but walk up and down
this hallway. faces watch from doors.

I was admitted for trying to
kill myself. did it really help?

"when did the city make you so cold?"

lonely bridges of concrete
and ice. knee-deep in slush and snow.
exposed flesh stinging from wind. lashes
freeze. almost blind. frigid journeys
from your bed to mine.

lost in the tide (I want you to dive out of your skin)

you have receded too far into yourself. the petrel
of your soul has been battered by icy winds,
swept to awful places, and those tiny wings
will never be able to take you home.
there is only

(.yako ton era uoy tub)
the ocean, ominous and unpredictable,
(diarfa regnol on era uoy .nettogrof)
lashing at you and attempting to pull
(eb ot sevaw eht rednu uoy)
you under the waves to be
(llup ot gnitpmetta dna uoy ta gnihsal)
forgotten. you are no longer afraid
(,elbatciderpnu dna suonimo ,naeco eht)
but you are not okay.

**I remember the colour of the sky
the day our worlds drifted together.**
-- for S.

enthralled with life, you marvel
at the nucleus within every cell.

unwavering, your belief in our
power to change ourselves
could move mountains.

each breath emanates passion,
hovering in the air like phosphenes,
or clouds of swirling fireflies.

the price of my skin

caress.
devour.

flesh plucked like the petals of a flower.

fill me with your need;
one that matches my hunger;
too much for you alone to bear.

I shudder -- pulled apart betwixt
a flurry of desperate and eager hands.

the shame has built a room
and I still live there.

your teeth are fine, a light will shine

do not be afraid of the darkness.
sit with it. let it wash over you.

acknowledge that it will always be there.
acknowledge that it has no power over you.

Kintsugi

I collect the shards of my being.
they do not fit quite together.
I rearrange them; improve
upon my initial design.

I fill these cracks with gold.
they do not define me, but
refine me -- more resilient
and brilliant than ever
before.

abaddon

a lifetime of digressions and disappointments stalk me with insatiable hunger. they usher me along a series of corridors and rooms. no sense of direction -- threatened by apoplexy. each turn leads me farther away from where I need to be. whispers become howls, cacophonous, throwing atypical patterns down the hallways. I quicken my pace. it is only a matter of time before I falter. when they finally pass over me there will be no trace, and this place will once again be vacant and still.

halcyon days

latch onto those times
when life seemed to float
by, like feathers drifting
down from the sky.

scattered amongst years
of illness, buried by time
and trauma, they remain
to be rediscovered:

reminders of how
to feel loved, and
to share that love
with others.

let them strengthen
your resolve:

building walls around us
as quickly as they erode.

An undying shadow

sweat drips down my face
as I sit in my living room,
trying to survive another
humid night.

the spectre of suicide waits
with me, mocking me as
I drag myself through
the agonizing hours.

I plug my ears with wax
to block out its horrid voice.
I tape blinders to my glasses
to hide its ghastly form.

I see it in mirrors and I stab
it repeatedly but it never dies.

Solace

in this cavern of your remains I urge you to dwell no longer.
along the skull's inner plate, etch your favourite memory:
it will outlast earth and bone, shimmering amongst countless
others. become one with them and learn your true name.

II.

"my blood is not that colour anymore."

Ihavechosentowalkdownadifferentroad.thepotholesin
thisonewillbreakmyankles.Ihavechosentowalkdownadi
fferentroad.thepotholesinthisonewillbreakmyankles.Ih
avechosentowalkdownadifferentroad.thepotholesinth

I have chosen to walk down a different road.
the potholes in this one will break my ankles.

isonewillbreakmyankles.Ihavechosentowalkdownadif
ferentroad.thepotholesinthisonewillbreakmyankles.Ih
avechosentowalkdownadifferentroad.thepotholesint
hisonewillbreakmyankles.Ihavechosentowalkdownad
ifferentroad.thepotholesinthisonewillbreakmyankles.

disability.

the coke cans pile up.
the dishes pile up.
the medications pile up.
the failures pile up.

wilt

commit to starving. it will only take
a month. less if you are parched.

no ghost in this machine

schizoaffective disorder is eating me alive.
skin pale like fluorescent light. give me pills
to ease the pain that burns inside my brain.

slowly withering away.

no more will to speak.
no ghost in this machine.

**do not touch me with those hands, with orifices
vomiting a series of progressively smaller hands.**

another sleepless night. the room spins round and round.
every noise is a danger lurking in the dark -- a creak
in the stairs -- the faint wail of the wind.

people crawl across the floor; they stare at me
with scarecrow faces while wrapping me in silk
that smells and feels like old hay.

Ziprasidone

your subsistence is dissipating
faster than you could ever imagine.

when did everything become so despondent?
your mind will unravel beyond the constraints of
psychotherapy.

there is nothing for you here.
there is nothing for you here.
there is nothing for you here.

will this frac/tured world which you perceive
ever consign to order and peace?

mutism

words falter and expire in my larynx.
I feel like I just repeat myself repeat myself repeat myself
I beat myself into composure so that I can sustain a
conversation without having a fucking mental breakdown.

can't you hear those screams? can't you
see the shadows moving on the wall?

self-harm

I had to put all my cutlery in a box.

I locked it and threw away the key.

all I eat with now are plastic spoons.

the thought machine

scarecrows have built a machine. they hook it up to my brain with wires. it transmits images and thoughts about dying until I am numb. unable to do anything but fixate on the piles of dust collecting in the corners of my room.

we are luminous beings.

when

a

star

dies

it

takes

on

a

new

form

.

psychosis and summer rain

sedate and restrain me. I convulse with disdain.
arrythmic pulse. illness whispers in my blood.

impatient voices scrape and thunder in my ears:

"just kill yourself, already."

progress.

I haven't cut myself in fifteen months.
I finally cleaned my dishes after two years.
I'm still madly in love.

I still want to commit suicide.

your singing changes your voice.

I have started to accept my reflection.

I'm taking six medications, and this illness
that ruins everything has been wearing
thin; sunlight is shining through.

I have been discovering new dimensions to myself
and for once in my life, I'm excited.

IN SICKNESS AND IN DEATH

I.

a world, in me, in a world, in me, in a world...

inside
of
myself

.

away from myself

Pregabalin (February)

Anxiety storms.

suffocating.

trapped inside.

February rain

soaks into my bones.

teeth chattering.

legs shaking.

shivering.

cold sweat.

pills consumed

twice daily.

begging for relief.

The Light

I bought a gun last night
with every intent to end
my life.

hands shook as I slowly
loaded the cartridge,
took off the safety.

I sat there for twelve
hours. how am I supposed
to do this? through
the temple?

should I put the barrel
in my mouth? I tried,
tasted the cold metal.

my finger floated
above the trigger.

in the end, I couldn't
bring myself to do it.

under dawn's feeble
light I buried it.

maybe one day I will have the strength.
beneath a red maple it waits for me.

bed sores

these days it's hard to stay alive.
these days I'm drying up inside.
I can't get out of my bed.
I can't get out of my head.

observation room 2

how many times
have I been here?
I have lost count.
it seems like fate.

how many days
will I rot?

with no sun
that shines,
no breeze
that cools,
no shower
to cleanse.

lights turned on and off
intermittently, depending
on the nurse's schedule.

a camera that watches
my every move, every
thought.

one day the doctor
will return, with a form
that I can sign,

stating that yes,
I am aware of myself,
I am no longer a harm
to myself or others,
I am safe to live
in society.

when I die will I return here?

my corpse in the bed, propped
up against the wall,
while they take blood samples
and ask me asinine questions
about my mood and lifestyle
habits.

August 18th, 2021

we sat next to each other
on the train from Windsor
to Toronto.

you complained
that the ride
was boring.

it was then that
you told me
about the miscarriage.

"in ten days it will
have been a year
ago."

you pointed to
the date on the
calender.
August 28th.

you held up
your hands to
approximate
its size.

"only a month early,
but it was so small."

you told me how
your husband
left you that day.

you told me about
your uncle's funeral
parlour, how you used
to have to help dress
the corpses; how the
family thought you
should be the one
to tend to it before
the cremation.

you complained that
the train ride was boring.

can you see me in your mind?

I   want   to   eat   your   brain

to

heal

mine

.

concrete children

I've resigned the cumbersome task of training the social animal. the infamous face of artificial concern is crudely stapled to our calcified mugs which are bitterly being filled with boiled and steeped bullshit from the exhausted hands of minimum wage desperation. drawn and quartered by the privileged: it's the age of consumption and the new mantra is "smoke flesh. eat kids."

we're all man-made, spilling thickly from construction rigs into moulds that are purposefully ill-equipped for the harsh frost that cakes our frames and seizes our very foundations; and all those concrete children are heaving and cracking under the pressure, and soon they will scream in such unanimity that it will blast a hole in Jericho's sky, through which our polluted ideals can drift into the farthest reaches of the galaxy like a cloud of toxic star dust, warping into deadly nebulae. the children are eroding, and their disintegrated fragments are being lost in translation until at last there are no more youthful attributes left: replaced by the avalanche of insects that fuck and feed and die in our brains.

In Sickness And In Death

I will follow you

I will worship you

I will live with you

I will learn from you

I will laugh with you

I will cry with you

I will die with you.

severe anhedonia.

dreams aren't worth chasing. textbooks and professors defecate jargon into my ears but it isn't registering. in fact, nothing is. all my senses have succumbed to a sickness which started in my brain, seeped into my blood, and my bones, and my skin, until it has completely assimilated into my being and I can't go on any longer.

"you could have been anything you wanted." "you're better than this." "don't throw your life away." "just keep your chin up." "it will get better." "think of all the people that love you." "everyone gets depressed at some point." "there's nothing wrong with you." "how could you do this to us?"

I'm leaving now.

laughing at the absurdity inherent to your optimism

my hobbies and artistic efforts are nothing
but ways to distract myself from the anguish
bestowed upon me by mental illness
and trauma.

this hole in my chest continues to grow.
[prescription breath / numb to the bone]
this hole in my chest is all I know.
[injecting death / still just as cold]

submerge

this excursion was doomed from the start.

unprepared for the pressure, our vessel groans
and creaks as bolts and valves come loose.

thrashing; gulping; mouthfuls of bitter truth.
sinking; gasping; choking on this abyss
that is reminiscent of you.

carried away to where the sky and sea
will cave into never-ending shades of blue.

Pulse

slowing every second
until but a faint trace
remains.

vision blurring. halos of
light all mingle into one.

speech is slurring. unable
to express a single world.

the empty pill bottle
falls from my slack
hand. my head tilts
back in indifference.

eyes stare blankly
as I wait for the grand
shape of my destroyer.

isolated; detached

depression and psychosis reign.
it's hard to discern what is reality.
suffering from this brain abnormality;
a malady with no known cure or remedy.

I swallow eight pills daily, I receive an injection monthly,
all to make life slightly more bearable. mostly

I wonder why I bother getting out of bed.

"inevitably dark"

bitter. blunted. dismal. detached.
not a single fucking day without
a panic attack.

voices that berate me;
medications that sedate me.
mixed affective state —
euphoric, suicidal, irate.

retching from the stench of my
acrid breath as I dislodge
a torrent of yeti crabs from an acid
scorched throat. poverty and
scarecrow faces smother me.

retreating further from the strange
customs of social interaction.

descending into layers of unreality:

a hole through which my consciousness
shall become oblivious and, subsequently,

lost.

schizoaffective disorder is destroying me.

when will this end?

a ceaseless torrent of episodes

crash againt me like waves

carving away the cliffs

of my will.

this shall end when there
is nothing left of me.

drain flies

they have come

in torrents issuing

forth from my pipes.

I can't sleep at night.

soon they will devour

flesh,

      muscle,

           sinew.

"the skyscrapers look like gravestones from out here."

pacing aimlessly
through a maze of glass and concrete
graves.

the living dead reside
in every room; peering anxiously from
windows.

I can't bear their horrid gaze,
those paper-white faces,

the April snow.

the onset of sickness.

it was the onset of sickness: up from subconscious rivers
and into the valley, where husks of people slowly
wither from routine to afford the luxury of being
dumped into graves.

we all felt it; an ache that
sucked at the marrow of our bones.

the sun refused to rise, and the moon and stars
flickered and vanished. we yearned to see
the stars again.

no one went outside anymore...

and though we huddled together in a new world of silent
darkness, we had never felt so alone -- relentlessly mocked
from behind dismal windows until nowhere felt like home.

we turned on ourselves in desperation: seeking the refuge
of a rope in dim basements; or casting ourselves from
the cliff to a forgiving bed of rocks below...

a few still lurk about, pale in the silent darkness; it was
the onset of sickness, and we would never be the same.

apathy.

my life can be likened to a dying weed:
it used up all it could drain with its roots
and will wither away, unnoticed.

I never wanted it in the first place.

I don't get out of bed for any particular
reason. books are tiresome; art and music
are dull; faces are alien to me.

these days, I can't even
care enough to die.

misophonia

disgust.

rage.

panic.

the sound is driving me mad.

gnashing   (of teeth).
squelching   (of food).

the horrible chewing.

it will be the death of me.

phantoms / winter

the air is diminishing
frost in the absence
hypothermic dreams

there is a reason
that I am confined
to this husk of dullness
surrounded by phantoms.

they beseech me
to freeze my blood
and join them

in a macabre dance.

footprints in the snow
a steady rhythm of sickness
as they encircle me

anthropological discovery of a suicide

a man sits in ruin. his life falls apart around him. anguish churns in his stomach like a vat of rotten milk. his situation is made worse just thinking about it. after five days, he stands and scours the dirty kitchen for a knife; slits his throat; his body crumples to the floor. dust and structural collapse cover him like a shroud. buried, now, under six thousand years of dirt.

"we can't bear your illness anymore."

I'm sorry that I haven't been able to come to practice. I don't have money for the bus, and every time I cross that bridge all I can think of is jumping off into the falls.

"What would you have done if this never happened?"

can I imagine life without my disability?

yes, I fantasize about it every day.

it has become a fixation.

and yes, it furthers my desire to

k
i
l
l

m
y
s
e
l
f
.

I am just a container.

old, crumpled,
label peeled off;
my lid is nowhere to be found.

I am bent out of shape
because, day by day, my contents
have been removed by an ice cream
scoop.

there is nothing left in me
yet still some hungry being
grips me tight and scrapes along
my interior.

the force and determination of this apparatus
have pulled apart my seam which was already
starting to unglue.

soon, I will unfurl:
a long piece of cardboard coated in
spoiled and coagulated dairy film
which flakes off
in the wind.

a cold and unforgettable January afternoon

my whole life I have been
s t a l k e d
by shadows that blend
and change shape to haunt me.

pushing people away
with my despondency.

after years of wandering this dissonant place
that you would certainly deny as reality,
I have become unable to comprehend
anything else and I am forced to go
deeper into myself and I can't restrain
this madness anymore.

everything has led up to this moment:

as I stand here at the edge of this river
— cinder block held steady between
determined hands, looped around
my neck with a chain which bites
into flesh —

I prepare to plunge into those icy depths.

"funny," I thought,

"that this is how it will end. I always
detested the idea of drowning."

I remind myself that no one will ever find
the body, and of that, at least, I am glad.

the marrow of our bones

haematopoiesis produces 500 billion blood cells per day.

rejuvenate.

life flows freely from our bones.

II.

days. weeks. years.

remnants of yesterday bark from my broken stereo. fragments of static. lost in this room for days. weeks. years. the door (to a better tomorrow? or something worse?) is warped shut. it's never been used. bits of nail lodged into claw marks dragged across the floor.

Rorschach

I can't keep doing this
walking between the rain
the last thread of reality
has snapped

Rorschach patterns discovered
in the splatters of my brain on the wall.

dry; empty; mountain

old wounds torn open by fresh wounds.
with patience and dedication, I carry out
this procedure through day and night.

soon my whole body will be
covered in an armour of scars

scrawls upon a weary tomb/tome.

"**never shall I smile. never shall I die.**"

i.

depressive episodes that last
for months, sucking all delight
from my art, from writing, from
music. even friends and family
seem far away.

the hole in my chest
is taking everything
from me.

ii.

bursts of mania rip through
the darkness with lightning
and thunder. false elation.
racing thoughts. searing
anger. frivolous spending.
my brain is on fire.

when the fever subsides I witness, with
shame, the gravity of my actions.

iii.

psychotic waves wash
over me. my blood is
calling to me, begging
to be released.

I'm losing my grip
on reality; certain
that this sickness
will devour me.

there is no relief.

stabbing at these mirrors of regret.

frayed and looped rolls of film project
suicide, isolation, misery, guilt, avolition,
mania, apathy, disdain, etcetera.

March (Escitalopram)

wracked with despondency.
crawling through another day.

can't bear the weight of this
illness. grasping for a sense
of stillness.

depression has taken control.
exhaustion is taking its toll.

psychosis thrusts me deeper,
deeper into this hole.

Mimosa pudica

I tend to your soil

I water your roots

I bathe you in sunshine

I shelter you from storms

and yet, when I touch

your leaves, they

retract

ophthalmologist

the cysts have returned
a surgeon must remove them
before it's too late

there's blood in my tears
shying away from the light
until I have healed

an ode to nerve pain

searing.

shooting down my arm
like venom.

simple tasks
like lifting a glass
are excruciating.

can barely sit still.
laying down is
nearly impossible.

it has been thirteen weeks
and the agony persists.

an oblique reference to dying

a grim ritual; a cold blade sinks into flesh. shoulders sag; eyes close.

Chimera

you are lost in this city of salt: its buildings glimmer strangely while bathing in moonlight. fog from your breath obscures a silhouette. your sweat leaves footprints on the pavement in a residue of regret. the being comes closer -- an unsettling gait -- eyes that flicker in the dark.

it is not human. you can see three horrid faces. haunted by familiarity, you have been here before and return each night for it to drain more life from you. its mouths are open, pouring salt to sting your wounds. they will never heal until you escape this place.

banish this mirage. tying knots in its esophagus. it sputters clumps of melting hair. *banish this mirage.* white-knuckled in a stranglehold. fingers splinter from the force. *banish this mirage.* your neck is sore. winter morning cough. *banish this mirage.*

absolved.

this home shall become my grave.

shoveling poverty and sickness
over a coffin of guilt.

**my illness was slowly revealed to me
like a blossoming flower**

sick and tired of being sick and tired. I did not wake up one day destroyed, but from years of numbing exposure to degrading voices that integrate into daily thought patterns: *"I'm useless." "I'm a burden." "I should disappear."*

turn to stone and wear away.

devour

slinking away from the day.
knees and palms are raw.
I have nothing more to say.
I am being consumed
by dejection's maw.

unlike Prometheus,
what has been lost
will not regenerate
in the morning.

cicada

buried beneath the soil
for seventeen years.

when I emerge it takes
a moment for my eyes
to adjust to the sun.

I cry out in that tone that
is ever so familiar to you;
a song to herald warmer
days.

a separation from the self.

Yesterday I didn't know who or where I was. None of my belongings evoked memories when I looked at them or held them. I walked around the apartment as though in a stranger's home and I didn't recognize myself in mirrors or pictures. Today I feel I'm not real; just a bad dream that people are tired of having and would be better off waking up from.

Metastasis

erosion reveals the spirit. let it radiate, pour into empty spaces. leave this lonely city where dreams go to die and the rent is too high.

Nosferatu

the vampire at my door
beckons me to turn
the lock and let it in.

I can feel my will
slipping away.

soon it will be upon me,
drinking the last of my essence
until I am one of them.

there is no blood left
in my veins, yet
still my heart beats.

pillar of salt

don't. look. back.

grapple with the temptation that sparks
throughout every cell in your body.

don't. look. back.

accept the absence.
it will help you discover
yourself while climbing
rocks with fervent
jubilation.

don't. look. back.

leave the past to rot in the inferno.

**distorted fragments of conversations
we've already had**

c a n

   y o u

survive

the

    i s

d   t
     a
  n
 c
 e

  ?

**may all that has been reduced to noise
in you become music, again**

the static of suicide screeches,
scrapes along my eardrums.

incessant. unbearable. nothing can drown
it out. it seeps into me, eroding every
beautiful note. it follows me wherever I go.

it exacerbates my daily need to die.
it greets me each morning
and tucks me in at night.

electroconvulsive therapy
recommended for the third
time in my life.

I live in constant fear,
with that awful sound to
remind me that I am never
alone.

Helianthus
— for K.

Elysian fields bathed in gentle hues of yellow and green are reflecting vividly behind eyes shut tight. an entire existence dedicated to prepare for this excursion beyond the self. visage embraced by a mask of woven cloth. in the fabric's ancient palate, a reticent tongue explores the taste of rebirth. a ritual to burn this weathered shell. mortal clay loses shape (features cascade). consciousness retained in roots and leaves. discover the colour of your dreams.

the mind outlives the body. wake to these helianthus fields.
the mind outlives the body. facing east, waiting for the dawn.

goodnight ghosts only I can see

they stalk me
from room to room,
pace aimlessly
up and down my hallway.

soiled clothes. weathered, dirty skin.
greasy hair and breath like heroin.

I live with them. we play games where we
pretend that each of us doesn't exist.

if you're quiet, if you press your ears against the wall, you can still hear him humming.

do not mourn my passing;
be glad that I am finally

free.

the embarrassment of living

people tell me,
"but you were doing so well."

as though my illness were not chronic,
a lifelong journey of sickness and recovery.

as though schizoaffective disorder were
something you simply wake up okay from one day.

as though the hallucinations
were mere blips on a map
that magically vanish
with medication.

as though the thought disorder
did not interfere with writing
even this poem.

as though the manic episodes
did not stab into me like the thrust
of a knife.

as though the depression did not
slowly erode my foundation, returning
each time more powerful and complete.

as though the suicidality did not seep
into everything, threatening my life
on a daily basis.

I can't cook. I can't clean.
I can't work. I can't sleep.
I can't love or start a family.

all the things that make us human
are slowly being robbed from me.

hungry / ghosts

It's all over
they are on the march
and lo, death was left
in their wake;

their never ending desire
to stay alive.

the need to construct a new reality

I.

Kaiju

demolish everything in sight.
loved ones and strangers
turn in fright.

how many people stood
on the bridges you've burned?

delusions of worthlessness
trample every future.
watch them crumble.

I can no longer live like this:
desperate and in despair.

giving spatial dimensions to an entity
that has come to destroy my world.

Hunger

the fridge is empty.
the cabinets, too.

I must suffer through this hunger.

four days until I get paid.
only water to sustain me.
onset of muscle fatigue.

I must suffer through this hunger.

I hang my stomach around
my neck like an albatross.
my private penance.
yes, I deserve this.

I must suffer through this hunger.

December (you are gone but your light still shines)
— for K.

I cling to the memories.
try to remember your smell.

forget those shaky hands,
downward stares,
heavy sighs.

instead I relish in your smile;
the warmth of your embrace;
the comfort of your words.

without you I would have died.

each day that I am on the brink
I remind myself of you;
think of sunflowers;

somehow
live
another
day.

Piledriver

the weight of this disorder:
it falls upon me.
decimating.
obliterating.

my knees buckle
as I trudge
towards the abyss.

voices chuckle
as I stumble.

the weight of this disorder:
it falls upon me.
decimating.
obliterating.

my concrete skin
splinters from the pressure.
my confidence
eliminated by this profound
despondency.

dissociate.
dissociate.
dissociate.
dissociate.

an ode to B.S. Johnson

I yearn to travel back in time

find your lonely self and shower
you with adulation.

I wish to kiss your wrists, pour
the blood back into your veins.

relax, it won't be okay.

do you have a suicidal fantasy?
like twitching in the snow in the fits of an overdose?
or have you never been defeated by illness?

I'll do it on my birthday / a gift for you all.

perpetual implosion

suffocating.
like a planet falling
into a black hole.

it is endless, it is cold, and it is crushing you.

succour

craving silence: driven mad by the incessant hum of the refrigerator; the hush of passing cars on wet asphalt; the blackness that pulses through veins, expanding and contracting with each sullen breath, condensing in my bones as they turn to lead. hot and cold flashes. a blur of half-remembered moments bubbling to the surface, reminding me of everyone I love and all the times I've hurt them. disgusted that I'm even writing this, as if my misery were special; as if there weren't billions of people suffering in unfathomable ways, hinted at by the bruises that the girl down the street tries to cover up with a foundation which doesn't quite match her pale complexion. I want to tell her that one day all this will end, but I can't -- words lodge in my throat, the bubbles of thought now a vapour searing away everything except the dull ache that throbs *(rhythmically, relentlessly)* in the centre of my chest.

the paranoia machine

I swear they are laughing
at me from inside the walls.

"what a failure."

"he can't even leave his apartment."

*"and have you looked at the place?
what a fucking dump."*

"his writing is a disgrace, too."

"ten bucks says he won't last another year."

"the end is built into the beginning."

we lay together in this house,
the one I moved into many
years ago.

it is perpetually in flames.

I know that it will be the death of me.

please, before the end,
hold me close, like you used to.

whisper in my ear
that you will never leave me.

my days are numbered.

mental hospital blues

each day I narrowly avoid death.

completely debilitated.

summoning the strength
to avoid that fucking hospital.

the arrival of autumn
— for A.

the leaves are wilted

falling slowly to the
ground like your
ashes.

can't stop thinking about
that dark night
when you left
this world.

twisted metal.
broken glass.

every now and then
I still hear your laugh.

Nine of Swords

I have drawn thee seven times.

Lord of Cruelty,
bestow your
curse upon me.

haunted by bad dreams.
illness lurking
around every corner.

mocked by visions of the psychiatric ward.
it is only a matter of time before I return.

"we were making castles in the sand.
now we swim in the sea that swept them away."

erosion of buildings:

sand turns to mud
before being swallowed
by the sea.

we must not mourn their loss:
it is a part of the neverending
cycle of creation, destruction,
and rebirth.

to be relieved of their structure
is to embrace the ebb and flow
of the waves, to swim freely
in the oceans of time and space.

floating, filled not with fear, but life.

overdose (Fluoxetine)

one.
hands eerily steady
as I begin to type
up my suicide note.

two.
head reeling with guilt
and misery and madness.

three.
feel the capsules slide
down my esophagus.

four.
start composing emails
for loved ones and people
I have wronged.
"do not open until after January 3rd."

five.
I miss my dogs.
I wonder if I'll see them
on the other side.

six.
I can't stop crying.

seven.
at least I won't hear
the voices anymore.

eight.
"what the fuck is wrong with me?"

nine.
puke it all up into the toilet.

Event Horizon

these are the years of babies, marriage, and graduate degrees; friends that leave overseas. reminded constantly that others are achieving their dreams while I try to survive on disability and wonder why the fuck I wake up every day, because it's only getting worse: brain unraveling by the second, thoughts spilling and spluttering from every orifice.

I should have stayed in Ha Long Bay.

my spine has become twine. I twist it around
my eggshell parts but it's quickly splitting at the knot.

I had a batch of aspirations. not many have hatched;
most have been smashed, in fact, and I lament my lack
of tact when I try to reenact how I felt during those humid
days: when all time seemed to stop, and we were
surrounded by an ocean of mountains.

if I could, I would drag them to raise
your spirits; drain the sea and let it
rush into that growing space
between your shoulder blades.

I should have stayed in Ha Long Bay.

a house of shame (built for me with stones)

weeks of malnutrition split forth the trauma buried in your anus. hypnotized by the sloshing of blood and excrement, become lost in broken memories -- a fog of jeers and smirks as they slam your head against brick wall; face pressed into asphalt; feel them undoing your belt; hear the buckle clink against pavement; a faint voice that sounds like yours: *"please, stop."* dissociate for hours *(years)*. curl up on concrete. shiver. whimper. wait for numbness to limp you home.

Nocebo

I sit in an office with two psychiatrists. they tell me that my disorder is complicated. for three hours we discuss the fragments of my being, and which adhesives would be most effective. day hospital programs. group CBT and occupational therapy. medications. debt. empty stomach. the noose waiting patiently under my bed. strange faces on crowded buses. the cleaver grinning from my table.

I know that the services these doctors offer will amount to nothing, but I need something to fill the days. murmurs of agreement.

"we'll see you next week."

Ennui

scars deepen the pit in my gaze.
a veil is laid across
horizons, where each star
is another a grave.

**don't look at my fucking teeth
while I'm trying to talk to you.**

hiding from the dentist
like my receding gums.

enamel eroding
as quickly as my will.

broken molars leave
abrasions on my tongue.

acid reflux; a sour
taste in my mouth

where yet another word
is caught, chewed, swallowed.

psychic venom

starved and abandoned at the precipice of existence.
I pray for the serpent tongue to annihilate my being.

II.

"swim and swear you shall reach the pain."

salt makes me gag.
I've been swimming
for hours. no sign
of the shore.

even the birds don't
come out this far.

arms and legs on fire.
eyes stinging red.

no end in sight.

for now, it is
enough that
I am alive.

galvanize

I will not be weathered.

I refuse to oxidize
in the presence
of this disorder.

coat me in zinc to
shelter me from storms.

shock me until
I don't care
about dying.

requiem

sifting through failed dreams. there is no longer a reason to get up in the morning. I lay down one last time. dirt rains from the sky. scraping of shovels. muffled condolences.

"the nightmare is over."

The Devil

"that which is predetermined but is not for this reason evil."

my illness comes custom made
but it was not crafted by a malicious
being.

no.

it is simply the product of faulty wiring.
bad genetics.

my brain is different from yours.

I see and hear and think
things that would curdle
your blood like milk.

people call my ability to express my
suffering a gift. maybe they are right.

but

to me, creation is simply
a necessity for survival.

waiting for more rejection letters.

I admire your willpower
in the face of disquiet.

yet I find it difficult
to be absorbed
by your pages.

talking around
your anguish.

it takes you a paragraph
to say, *"I am unwell."*

tedious traces of you
flitter between sentences.

words pacing in circles —
frivolous, endless circles.

more lights in the city than the sky

when was the last time we were truly able to see an astrological event?

every time there is an eclipse, or meteor shower, the sky is either overcast or filled with light pollution.

you have to drive for miles outside of the city just to see the Perseids.

constellations traced in streetlights.

how do the animals navigate? can they still find their way home?

this is not my home.

sitting in darkness all
hours of the day. spitting
at the walls now flecked
with tar-soaked mucus.

there is no one here

just a ghost that wanders
from room to room in cramped,
anxious patterns.

at times like these I am
convinced that I have
been dead for years:

haunting this dismal place
in a futile attempt to find
my body which decomposed
decades ago.

**my voice is a bit off-key, but that's okay
(wailing words of worry, hope, and fury)**

I'm sick of cowering in bed;
hiding from things that I can not
change.

I'm sick of my tired body.
I used to be more than this.

I need to glue my black blues
back together; they're cracked
and the hues used to be much
lighter.

**I admire your Jesus Lizard collection,
but I can't feel anything anymore.**

unbuttoning my shirt,
I gaze upon your
canvases, and CD
collection, and remark
that your taste in music
is more eclectic than
the last painter
I fucked.

you laugh and pull
me to the bed;

*your fingers do not
hesitate as they brush
across the cuts on my
ribcage.*

you never mentioned them.
they didn't seem to matter.

I was grateful for that.

walking down St. Laurent,
the wind has picked up
and it's colder than usual
for late August.

as I pass the Rogers TV station
I remember that I haven't paid
my bills in a couple months.

affliction

mental illness is a persistent death
and I must admit that its obduracy
impresses me.

it's affecting my performance of daily tasks,
like eating and breathing and sleeping
and walking in a straight line. I fear it will
also affect the quality of my voice.

the day I can no longer utter a scream
from my larynx is the day that I die.

"the light that you search for is
 the light that you're searching with."

the power was within me
all along.

please, no more dead friends

the machine yells until it is
hoarse and wheezing.

pacing frantically,
unable to eat, or relieve
its bladder or bowels.

put down
before asphyxiation
could seize control.

grasping at the shape of everything

this inexorable death
pursues me down
the corridor of suicide.

my only hope is months,
perhaps years away.

will my heart give out?
will my mind collapse?

or will at last I summon
the strength to shatter
these walls?

"I don't know where I am, but I know my flesh"

after trying to die five times
I am fighting to stay alive.

my sixth attempt will be the last.

until then I want to laugh,
love, and walk in the light
of the sun.

**when you finally behold your true self
you can begin to live for the first time.**

I shall peel back the layers
of reality, folding them in
such a way so as to reveal
the Universe to itself.

theatre of cruelty.

shuffle off this living death.

shatter these mental barriers,
these filthy lenses through which
we have learned to see ourselves
and the world around us.

this is not life.

this is an illusion
in which we die
every day but
are never born.

"a bonfire of dreams"

within each spark
each ember

I see an aspiration,
a goal, a yearning.

each individual flame
burning brightly, together

but my flame, my dream,
will not be found here.

I am simply a stranger
who stopped to warm
up by the fire.

stepping, at last, out of this illusion

this world has failed me.

I yearn to open a portal
to a new one.

it is there: I have seen
glimpses of it in the
corners of my mind.

**"I shall for the first time give
things the shape of my will."**
— for Antonin Artaud

together we shall
stride, with heads
held high, through
the valleys of life
and death.

it is time to end this immense suffering.
it is time to construct a new reality.

the profound ecstasy of being

I.

we are all one being hurting itself, trying to love itself

a yearning for connection
consistently drives us away.

yet there are brief moments
of mutual understanding

when the cosmos
of our minds
drift together,
remembering
that we are

one.

deliverance

praying for the advent
of a treatment plan

that will deliver me
from myself
to myself

I desire

i.

to liberate my being
from these chains
and these phantoms
which never cease
to molest my mind
and spirit and body.

inhaling the sharp, brilliant scent of life

there is more than this suffering.

there is the fury of passion
the clinging of lovers
the mirth of laughter
the embrace of friends
the Fire of creation

the profound ecstasy of being.

death pangs

they pierce me.

lacerations, my bleeding
wrists my bleeding mind.

is there no escape?
each day and night
I writhe in agony
as these death
sensations

course through my veins
and smother my thoughts.

my soul is asphyxiating,
I must break the hands
gripping its throat.

I have grown tired of destroying myself.

self harm is a tedious ritual
that has outlived its usefulness.

I care not to mar my flesh, to let
my blood spill onto the floor
in useless spatters.

I remember how running water and
summer air would sting the wounds.

I remember the anxious
glances from friends and family.

I remember how with each cut I was not freeing myself,
but building yet another wall between me and myself,
between myself and the world.

on suicide

I have concluded
that, within me,
there is not truly
a wish to die.

these visions of death
presented to me
are illusions.

rather, there is
an agonizing
and inescapable
need to experience
myself, *my true self*,
in spite of the spectres

which haunt every
moment of my being.

Prometheus

open the endless doors within my mind,
bestow upon me the Fire of creation
such that I may craft images
of my suffering, my passion,
my glory.

I shall attempt to speak from my soul
and into the souls of others, so as
to make them understand
they are not alone.

I will attempt to honour your sacrifice,
it will not have been in vain,

and one day I shall slay the fowl
perpetually eating your liver.

a connection transcending flesh

I have accepted that our mortal lips
will never again join in union

that our flesh will no longer
become a blur of passion.

but our souls,
our minds,
our hearts,

still beat as one.

shatter the mirror to liberate the reflection's form

for years I was trying to escape myself.
now, I am a stranger in my own mind,

and I wish for nothing more
than to return to myself.

the throat of my soul

I shall vomit onto this page
all the contortions
and yearnings

contained within me.

"you're insane and you should kill yourself."

sometimes (often, in fact) I conclude that my thoughts and actions have been predetermined by the scarecrows, because it is they who organize my brain in this obtuse manner so why then is it not possible that these men of straw have fabricated my mind itself, perhaps even my body? the irony is haunting, scarecrows building people. but it is conceivable because I have seen the ways in which they manipulate my reality and the forms they can take, and maybe they do this to everyone and only I am enlightened...it's all a sick game to them, making us destroy ourselves. but if I cease to exist then I, too, can become a terrible shadow of misery and death to unleash all my dark desires upon them, just to watch them

fall apart as I have.

I don't need you

this is a simple reminder that I don't need you.

I don't need you [xif kciuq a tsuj er'uoy]
[uoy deen t'nod I] because you are ephemeral,
I won't remember you tomorrow.

I don't need you [evil ot live ruoy dna]
[uoy deen t'nod I] to be happy.

                      to tell me what and how to be
                                           [
                                           u
                                           o
                                           y

                                           d
                                           e
                                           e
                                           n

                                           t
                                           '
                                           n
                                           o
                                           d

                                           I
                                           ]

I
d
o
n
'
t
need you [em ot gnihton era uoy]

I don't need you. I don't need you. I don't need you.

"in hospitals we rust"

despite being suicidal
I refuse to go to the hospital.

I will not again be condemned
to pace that fucking hallway.

anguished faces watching from every door.
a vile excuse for food placed before us
three times a day.

the only sun shining through
grimy, shockproof windows.

showers that turn themselves off
every minute. bathrooms without
locks. screaming patients, all hours
of the night.

no. I refuse to stagnate within those walls.

instead I shall revel in the absoluteness
of my being.

II.

even within rot there is life.

pulsing fungi. scuttling insects.
creeping mould. yes, it thrives.

on creation

with my drawings,
I am not trying to show you
an image of real life. no,

what I strive for is a glimpse
into the inexorable suffering

and celebration

of my soul.

comfort

I wish to build a fire
around which all
the people of the earth

may sit, and perhaps
by staring into the fire,
through the fire,

they will see each other
for the first time.

pain(t)

gouache spills from my veins
and drips onto the canvas
in mesmerizing rhythms
and patterns.

there are many colours,
not just red. a polychromatic
river of me, my essence.

Earth

tectonic shifts
create rifts
but also mountains
and valleys.

quartz. biotite. feldspar.
I channel their essence

in order to feed
my indomitable will.

terraform

this wasteland
shall become a lush
forest.

Air

the planet's breath
becomes our breath.

sculpting stone
bending trees

uprooting houses in
a whirlwind of fury.

shapeless. impossible
to tame. indefatigable.

Water

you are a river

ever-flowing around
each obstacle laid
before you.

willfully rearrange yourself
to fit any situation.

most importantly,
sustain life.

Fire

it brings warmth.

it reshapes.

it destroys.

and in the ashes
of its wake:

rebirth.

"But this flesh is only the beginning and only abstraction, abstraction...abstraction."

these veins are rivers
leading to my future.

no tether

unrestrained
but
not unhinged.

giving myself in
to the path that
is carved by my
will.

nothing can stop me now.

"you will live many lives."

I have died several times.
and I have been reborn.

I desire

ii.

to live a normal life.
to be able to work,
and go to school,
and build a reality
for myself.

to learn to live
with my illness.

to at last be whole.

ship of Theseus

I am a being in constant flux.

parts of me have been here since the dawn of time.
others have been recently added, replaced, restored.

I am uncertain which pieces
are old and which are new. to be honest
it doesn't really matter.

all that matters is that my sails continue to draw wind,
that my hull is impenetrable, that my captain never tires.

I whip him with the knotted chord of my will.

a ritual to assassinate the false Self

the beings have blindfolded me
and lead me, with a chain around
my neck, further into the 10th
sub level of preposterousness.
I occasionally stagger and fall

to my knees. I know we are
treading on broken glass
but years of this death march
have numbed me from the pain.

at last the blindfold and chain
are removed. the beings have
formed a ritual circle.

and in the centre of this circle:
me.

or rather, an effigy,
twisted from all the absurd
spasms of life which have
led me to believe that this
simulacrum *is* me.

yet it is simply an idol.
and idols are a mere
perception of form,
separated and estranged
from the true thing.

in other words, *this is not me*.
and I must destroy it to return
to myself.

ECT

I pray that one day

under the spell
of anesthesia

they will pass
a small current
through my brain

in order to stimulate
neural pathways.

will I finally be shocked
out of this illusion?

will I be able to face
my true self, at last?

acknowledgments

"you make my chest implode" is a lyric by Dioramic

"shaking off futility" is a song by Tangled Thoughts of Leaving

"all the oceans we contain, coming to light" is a lyric by At The Gates

"...our hands battered by the clutch of holding on" is a quote from House of Leaves by Mark Z. Danielewski

"One Day All This Will End" is an album by Svalbard

"I'll give myself three days to feel better" is a lyric by Bright Eyes

"he dreamt of Bones last night. I dreame of the Sunne" is a quote from House of Leaves by Mark Z. Danielewski

"when did the city make you so cold?" is a lyric by Woods of Ypres

"my blood is not that colour anymore" is a lyric by Faith No More

"the skyscrapers look like gravestones from out here" is a lyric by Acid Bath

"Inevitably Dark" is an album by Xasthur

"What would you have done if this never happened?" is a song by Suffocate For Fuck Sake

"never shall I smile. never shall I die" is a lyric by At The Gates

"the end is built into the beginning" is a quote from Synecdoche, New York "we were making castles in the sand. now we swim in the sea that swept them away." is a quote from an interview with Ulver.

"swim and swear you shall reach the pain" is a lyric by Christ Agony

"that which is predetermined but is not for this reason evil." is a quote from The Pictorial Key to the Tarot by A.E. Waite

"the light that you search for is the light that you're searching with" is a lyric by Thief

"the shape of everything" is an album by SOM

"I don't know where I am, but I know my flesh" is a quote from Intersect by Ray Fawkes

"bonfire of dreams" is an episode of the anime Berserk

"I shall for the first time give things the shape of my will." is a quote by Antonin Artaud

"in hospitals we rust" is a lyric by EYEHATEGOD

"But this flesh is only the beginning and only abstraction, abstraction...abstraction" is a quote by Antonin Artaud

"you will live many lives" is a painting by James R. Eads

artwork by Graham Cwinn

author photograph by Shannon Duncan (Level Up Photography)

special thanks: Max, Liam, Savannah, Rosie, Jake, Reed, Sara H., Brendan, Maeve, Evan, Shannon, Sara Y., Kyle, John, Shawn, Dave, Blake, Julien, my family, and everyone else who has supported me during my darkest and brightest days.

Published by Things in my Chest
Copyright © Graham Cwinn 2023

ISBN: 978-1-9991444-6-3

thingsinmychest.com

about the author

Graham Cwinn is a writer, artist, and musician living in Ottawa, Ontario. He has self-published several poetry collections, and is writing and illustrating a graphic novel. Graham also runs the small press Things in my Chest. His work offers glimmers of hope in the face of schizoaffective disorder, trauma, and loss.

other books by Graham Cwinn

Tangled Thoughts of Leaving
hiraeth - listen carefully to hearts breaking.
Crawl Inside
"one day all this will end."
the flesh is not a prison
my neighbour wants to kill me